This book is dedicated to my firm's clients, who make a lasting difference in the lives of people every day. Your excellent work and your encouragement are an inspiration to me and to my entire team. I am especially grateful to those of you who trusted me with significant professional responsibilities very early in my career. I will always remember that.

UNRELATED BUSINESS INCOME AND THE CHURCH

The Concise and Complete Guide™

MICHAEL E. BATTS

The contents of this publication do not constitute legal, financial, accounting, tax, or any other type of professional advice. For professional advice regarding the subject matter addressed herein, the services of a competent professional should be obtained.

Accountability
Press

www.accountabilitypress.com

in cooperation with

BMWL | BATTS
MORRISON
WALES & LEE
CERTIFIED PUBLIC ACCOUNTANTS

www.nonprofitcpa.com

ISBN: 1-4662-1370-1
ISBN-13: 978-1-4662-1370-8

Acknowledgment

I would like to acknowledge and thank Michele Wales, one of my fellow shareholders in our CPA firm, Batts Morrison Wales & Lee, P.A., for her significant contributions to this book. Michele coordinates our tax practice for nonprofit organizations and provided invaluable input for this project.

Table of Contents

Introduction

The purpose of this book

This book was written to provide church leaders with an easy-to-read, nontechnical, and concise guide to unrelated business income for their organizations. Church leaders need accurate information in order to make informed decisions. There are numerous technical tax guides available that offer excellent and thorough technical information on the topic, complete with citations of the Internal Revenue Code, Treasury Regulations, court cases, and IRS rulings. This book is not intended to be such a treatise. In writing this book, I have sifted through the Code, Regulations, cases, and rulings in order to provide an executive summary to help busy church leaders in their decision-making.

501(c)(3) public charity edition of this guide

A separate edition of this guide for 501(c)(3) public charities is available from Accountability Press (www.accountabilitypress.com). Although churches are also public charities under federal tax law, certain rules apply uniquely to churches. This book includes church-specific examples and addresses the special rules that apply uniquely to churches.

Myths and fables!

Many myths and fables surround the topic of generating unrelated business income...from "**you can't do that, it's illegal!**" to "**if you do that, you will lose your tax-exempt status!**" This book lays those myths and fables to rest with clear, no-nonsense information that not only tells you what you can't do, but more importantly, tells you what you can do, and how you can do it!

Alternative sources of tax-free income

My favorite part of this book is Chapter 5, which is entitled "Generating Income from Activities without Generating Unrelated Business Income." Most churches can benefit from additional sources of revenue. Chapter 5 provides clear information on a variety of alternative income sources that are not taxable!

1
Unrelated Business Income – The General Rules

Federal law imposes an income tax on a church if the church generates net income from one or more unrelated business activities. Congress adopted the tax on unrelated business income ("UBI") primarily for the purpose of eliminating unfair competition between nonprofit, tax-exempt organizations and for-profit, taxable businesses.

An unrelated business activity is a revenue-generating activity that:

- Constitutes a trade or business;

- Is regularly carried on; and

- Is not substantially related to the charity's exempt purposes.

The law also considers the activity of generating income

from "debt-financed property" to constitute an unrelated business activity. (See Chapter 3 for additional information on this topic.)

What constitutes a trade or business?

For purposes of the tax on UBI, a trade or business generally includes any activity carried on for the production of income from the sale of goods or performance of services. Ordinarily, a church must have a motive (but not necessarily its primary motive) of generating profit from an activity in order for the activity to be considered a trade or business. Most fundraising activities would meet the definition of a trade or business, since fundraising activities are generally conducted for the purpose of generating additional funds for the church.

Example: A church sells T-shirts in connection with its theme of evangelism for the year. Each shirt costs the church $8.00 and the church sells them to its congregation for $7.00 each. The T-shirt selling activity is not carried on for the production of income and is not, therefore, a trade or business.

Example: A church sells Christmas trees to the public in a high-traffic area during the period leading up to the Christmas holiday. The church conducts this activity each year for the purpose of raising money for its youth ministry. Christmas trees are generally sold for approximately twice the church's cost. The activity of selling Christmas trees is a trade or business, because one of the church's motives is to generate income from the activity.

When is an activity regularly carried on?

In determining whether an activity conducted by a church is regularly carried on, the frequency and continuity of the activity must be addressed. If the activity is of a type normally conducted by taxable, for-profit businesses, the frequency and continuity of the church's activity is compared to the industry norm. An activity will generally be considered to be regularly carried on if the church conducts the activity with a frequency and continuity that is similar to that of the industry.

Example: A church conducts an annual bake sale in connection with a county fair that is held each year. At the bake sale, which is open to the public, a variety of cakes, cookies, pastries, and other similar products are promoted and sold. The sale and fair last two weeks each year. In addressing the frequency and continuity of the activity, the church compares its annual bake sale to the activities of the retail baking industry and with retail stores that sell baked goods. The church's activity is conducted for two weeks each year, while the industry norm for taxable businesses is to conduct their activities year-round. Even though the church's bake sale is conducted every year, it is not conducted with a frequency or continuity that is similar to the business industry norm. Therefore, the church's annual bake sale is not regularly carried on.

Example: A church sells Christmas trees to the public in a high-traffic area during the period leading up to the Christmas holiday. The church conducts this activity each year for the purpose of raising money for its youth ministry. In addressing the frequency and continuity of the activity, the church compares its annual Christmas tree sale to the activities of for-profit businesses that sell Christmas trees. The for-profit businesses generally sell Christmas trees at the same time of year and for approximately the same duration of time as does the church. The church's Christmas tree-selling activity is regularly carried on.

How does the church determine whether an activity is substantially related to its exempt purposes?

A revenue-generating activity is not considered to be substantially related to a church's exempt purposes merely because the income generated from the activity is used to fund the church's exempt purpose activities. In order to support the position that an activity is substantially related to a church's exempt purposes, the church must show that the conduct of the activity itself (and not the money from it) contributes importantly to the accomplishment of the church's exempt purposes.

In making this determination, the church must first identify its exempt purposes. This often-overlooked area of the law is extremely important. Most churches (and their tax advisors) assume that their exempt purposes are obvious and that the general concept of having a religious purpose is adequate. However, according to IRS Regulations, in determining whether an activity contributes importantly to a church's exempt purposes, the IRS looks to "the purposes for which exemption is granted." Accordingly, a church should be very deliberate when it comes to defining the exempt purposes for which it exists. Some of a church's purposes may be religious, some may be educational, and others may be charitable. The church itself establishes the purposes for which it exists, and such purposes are often stated in the church's governing documents (articles of incorporation or charter and bylaws). A church's stated exempt purposes should be drafted broadly so as to include all of its intended purposes and not merely the most common activities of a local church. A church with a more broadly-worded purpose statement will be better able to defend a broader array of revenue-generating activities as contributing importantly to its exempt purposes.

>*Example:* An example of a *narrowly-worded* church purpose statement is:

>This corporation shall have as its purpose the gathering of a congregation of believers dedicated to the worship and service of Almighty God.

>*Example:* An example of a more *broadly-worded* church purpose statement is:

>This corporation is dedicated exclusively to charitable, religious, educational, scientific, and literary purposes. This corporation's primary purpose is to reach people with the Christian Gospel message and to disciple Christian believers by and through as many methods and means as possible (including by conduct of public worship; conduct of missions activities; educational activities; creation, sale, and distribution of Christian media; conduct of Christian events; and other related activities) so as to maximize the number of people who may be reached and discipled for the glory of Almighty God. In addition to its primary purpose, the church has the following additional purposes:

- *Fostering an appreciation for and participation in the performing arts, recognizing that the arts are a gift from Almighty God;*

- *Serving the needs of the poor, the needy, the outcast, the sick, the widowed, and the elderly;*

- *Fostering adequate education among both the young and the old; and*

- *Conducting other activities in keeping with the Great Commission.*

In addition to establishing a sufficiently broad purpose statement, the church should ensure that the relationship between each of its revenue-producing activities and its purposes is clear. In some cases, such as selling Bibles and other overtly religious literature, the relationship may be obvious. In cases where the relationship is not obvious, the church should maintain documentation to support the relationship.

> **Example:** *A church sells decorative candles in its bookstore during the Christmas season. The church should create and maintain a document approved by a leader of the church with respect to its candle sales stating that the sale of candles in the Christmas season facilitates the celebration and reverence of Christ's birth and the message of hope and deliverance that He brought to earth. The document supports the church's position that the sale of candles contributes importantly to the church's exempt purposes. The document should*

make specific reference to the stated exempt purpose(s) supported by the activity.

Activities that include some related and some unrelated elements

A church may engage in revenue-generating activities that include some elements that are substantially related to its exempt purposes and others that are not. For example, the church may operate a bookstore that sells Bibles and religious books along with cosmetics. The fact that an activity (such as operating a bookstore) includes both unrelated and related elements does not cause the entire activity to be considered unrelated to the church's exempt purposes. Federal tax law applies a "fragmentation" rule that requires such activities to be separated into their related and unrelated elements. In this example, the sale of cosmetics would be considered <u>not</u> substantially related to the church's exempt purposes, while the sale of Bibles and religious books would be substantially related.

Examples of unrelated business activities

Unrelated business activities in a church may include:

- Operating a public restaurant;

- Operating a revenue-generating parking lot;

- Selling non-religious items in a bookstore (such as computers, cosmetics, and popular secular books);

- Providing administrative services to other unrelated organizations for a fee;

- Conducting travel tours that are not adequately religious or educational in nature; or

- Selling advertising in the church's newsletter.

A church is permitted to conduct an *insubstantial* amount of unrelated business activity. If a church engages in a *substantial* amount of unrelated business activity, the church could lose its tax-exempt status under Section 501(c)(3) of the Internal Revenue Code. (See Chapter 4 for a discussion of how much unrelated business activity is too much.)

2
Specific Exclusions from Unrelated Business Income

Federal law provides a number of specific exclusions from the tax on unrelated business income. While there are some exceptions with respect to how certain of the exclusions apply, income from the following sources is generally excluded from UBI:

1. Dividends, interest, annuities, capital gains, and other investment income;

2. Gains from the sale of property other than inventory;

3. Royalties;

4. Rent from real property;

(*Note: For income of the types listed in 1 - 4 above, the exclusion does not apply if the income is "debt-financed income" as described in Chapter 3. Also, special rules apply if interest, annuities, royalties, or rents are received from an entity that is controlled by the organization receiving the income. Churches should consult highly experienced tax counsel to assist in addressing the tax implications of such arrangements.)*

5. A trade or business in which substantially all of the work is performed by persons who are not compensated for their work (the "volunteer exception");

6. A trade or business conducted primarily for the convenience of the church's members, students, officers, or employees (the "convenience of members exception");

7. A trade or business that consists of selling merchandise, substantially all of which was received by the church as gifts or contributions (the "donated goods exception");

8. Qualified sponsorship activities; and

9. Bingo games that meet certain criteria (the "bingo games exception").

The volunteer exception

Under the volunteer exception (item 5 above), a trade or business is not an unrelated business activity if "substantially all" of the work in conducting the activity is performed by persons who are not compensated. The law is not specific as to the definition of "substantially all." However, court cases and rulings on the issue indicate that 85 percent or more of the hours of work constitutes "substantially all" of the work for this purpose.

> *Example:* A church operates a coffee shop in a retail location that is open to the public. The coffee shop is a trade or business that is regularly carried on and its operation is not substantially related to the church's exempt purposes. The coffee shop is operated entirely by unpaid church volunteers, although a minimal amount of work (less than 10 percent) is performed by the church's accounting staff related to the store's recordkeeping. Even though the operation of the coffee shop would ordinarily be an unrelated business activity, the fact that substantially all of the work in conducting the activity is performed by volunteers causes the coffee shop not to be an unrelated business activity.

The convenience of members exception

Under the convenience of members exception (item 6 above), a trade or business is not an unrelated business activity if it is conducted primarily for the convenience of the church's members, students, officers, or employees. For this purpose, court cases and rulings have interpreted the term "members" to include people who attend or participate in a church's worship services or other activities, regardless of whether they are actually members of the church.

> *Example:* A church operates a coffee and pastry kiosk during worship services and other events held at the church's facilities in order to provide refreshments to those attending or participating in the events. Even

if operation of the coffee and pastry kiosk meets the ordinary criteria to be an unrelated business activity, it will be excluded in this case, since it is conducted primarily for the convenience of the church's "members."

The donated goods exception

Under the donated goods exception (item 7 above), a trade or business of selling merchandise is not an unrelated business activity if "substantially all" of the merchandise sold was donated to the church. Court cases and rulings indicate that "substantially all" for this purpose means 85 percent or more of the merchandise sold.

Example: A church operates a thrift shop in a retail location on Main Street. The store is open six days per week on a schedule comparable to that of other retailers in the area. The store's workers are all paid employees of the church. Virtually all of the items sold in the thrift shop are items received by the church as donations. The shop also sells a few items of new clothing because the church is able to purchase and sell those items at a substantial discount. Sales of purchased inventory comprise approximately five percent of the shop's total sales. The church's operation of the thrift shop is not an unrelated business activity because substantially all of the shop's sales consist of merchandise donated to the church.

Qualified sponsorship activities

Revenue received by a church as payment for a qualified sponsorship activity (item 8 above) is not unrelated business income. A qualified sponsorship activity is an activity in which an outside party (typically a business) pays a church to sponsor an event or activity conducted by the church and receives in exchange certain limited types of recognition or acknowledgment. As long as the acknowledgment or recognition made by the church of the sponsor meets certain criteria, and the church does not provide the sponsor with a "substantial return benefit," the transaction constitutes a qualified sponsorship activity.

Permissible recognition

The following information about a business sponsor may be displayed, used, recognized, and acknowledged by the church as part of a qualified sponsorship arrangement:

- Name;

- Logos or slogans that do not contain qualitative or comparative descriptions of the sponsor's products, services, facilities, or company;

- Product lines;

- The fact that the sponsor is an exclusive sponsor of all or part of an event or activity;

- A list of locations, telephone numbers, or Internet addresses;

- Value-neutral descriptions, including displays or visual depictions, of the sponsor's product-line or services; and

- The sponsor's brand or trade names and product or service listings.

Federal regulations state that logos or slogans that are an established part of a sponsor's identity are not considered to contain qualitative or comparative descriptions. Additionally, the display or distribution of a sponsor's product by the sponsor or the church to the general public at the sponsored activity is permissible.

Advertising is not permissible recognition

Advertising provided by the church in exchange for payment is considered a "substantial return benefit" and is not permissible recognition. For this purpose, the term advertising means any message which is broadcast or otherwise transmitted, published, displayed, or distributed and which promotes or markets any trade or business, or any service, facility, or product. Advertising includes messages containing qualitative or comparative language, price information or other indications of savings or value, an endorsement, or an inducement to purchase, sell, or use any company, service, facility, or product. A single message that contains both advertising and an acknowledgment is advertising.

Acknowledgments provided to a business in a church's newsletter, magazine, or other regularly distributed periodical in exchange for payment are not permissible acknowledgments in a qualified sponsorship arrangement. A program or brochure produced and distributed in connection with a specific event is not a periodical for this purpose, and acknowledgments in such a document may be permissible recognition if they meet the criteria set forth above.

Payments for exclusive provider rights are not qualified sponsorship payments

If a church agrees to permit a business to be the exclusive provider of certain types of products or services in connection with the church's activities or events in exchange for a payment, the payment received by the church for the value of that benefit is not a qualified sponsorship payment.

Payments in excess of the value of substantial return benefits

Payments by a sponsor that exceed the fair value of substantial return benefits constitute qualified sponsorship payments if the applicable criteria are met.

> **Example:** *A business pays a church $20,000 to sponsor a weekend retreat for married couples. The church provides the business with advertising valued at $12,000 in exchange for the payment. Except for the advertising, all other benefits provided to the business in connection with the arrangement are permissible benefits in a qualified sponsorship arrangement. $8,000 of the payment by the business is a qualified sponsorship payment.*

Special note about arrangements that do not meet criteria for qualified sponsorships

If a church receives a payment in a transaction that does not meet the criteria for a qualified sponsorship payment, the income to the church is not automatically unrelated business income. The transaction would need to be evaluated in light of the definition of unrelated business income in order for that determination to be made. For example, if the church received payment from a business in an arrangement where the church endorsed the business at one event, one time, the payment may not constitute unrelated business income to the church, since the activity is not regularly carried on.

> *Example:* First Church has a Family Fun Weekend in October of each year. The event consists of a variety of entertainment, games, and other activities. Big Car Dealer enters into a sponsorship agreement with the church in which Big Car Dealer pays the church $20,000. In exchange for the payment, First Church agrees to prominently display Big Car Dealer's name and logo throughout the event and distribute flyers expressing gratitude to Big Car Dealer for its sponsorship and listing its location, website address, and the types of automobiles sold by the dealership. Additionally, First Church agrees to permit Big Car Dealer to park four of its new vehicles at the entrance to the event. The church provides no other benefits to Big Car Dealer. The income of $20,000 received by First Church in this transaction is a qualified sponsorship payment and is not unrelated business income to First Church.

> *Example:* The same facts apply as in the previous example, except that in addition to the benefits provided by the church in that example, the church also agrees to permit Big Car Dealer to be the exclusive sponsor of the event. No other businesses are permitted to sponsor the event. The result is the same. The income received by First Church is not unrelated business income. Exclusive sponsorship is a permissible form of recognition in a qualified sponsorship arrangement.

> *Example:* First Church has a Family Fun Weekend in October of each year. The event consists of a variety of

entertainment, games, and other activities. In connection with the event, Great Cola Company pays First Church $10,000 (the fair market value) for the right to be the exclusive provider of beverages to the church for the event. The church agrees not to procure beverages from any other vendor for the event. The payment by Great Cola Company is not a qualified sponsorship payment because the exclusive provider benefit provided by the church is not a permissible benefit in a qualified sponsorship arrangement. The determination of whether the payment is unrelated business income to the church would have to be made based on the regular definition of unrelated business income and other possible exceptions.

The need for good tax counsel for significant sponsorship arrangements

If a church wishes to generate significant revenue from qualified sponsorship arrangements, it should engage legal counsel to draft a standard sponsorship agreement and tax counsel to ensure that the standard agreement complies with the requirements for qualified sponsorships. Failure to comply with the requirements of the law can cause all or part of the income from the activity to be taxable as unrelated business income to the church.

The bingo games exception

Bingo games are not considered unrelated business activities if they:

- Meet the legal definition of bingo;

- Are legal where they are played; and

- Are played in a jurisdiction where bingo games are not regularly offered by for-profit organizations.

A bingo game, as defined by Treasury Regulations, is:

A game of chance played with cards that are generally printed with five rows of five squares each. Participants place markers over randomly called numbers on the cards in an attempt to form a preselected pattern such as a horizontal, vertical, or diagonal line, or all four corners. The first participant to form the preselected pattern wins the game. As used in this section, the term "bingo game" means any game of bingo of the type described above in which wagers are placed, winners are determined, and prizes or other property is distributed in the presence of all persons placing wagers in that game. The term "bingo game" does not refer to any game of chance (including, but not limited to, keno games, dice games, card games, and lotteries) other than the type of game described in this paragraph.

Example: Sycamore Church conducts bingo games each Friday night in Busy City, in which people buy bingo cards and try to be the first contestant to fill a row of spaces on the cards when numbers are called. The winner of each game wins a prize that is distributed at the event. Bingo is legal in Busy City, but only for nonprofit organizations. Income from Sycamore Church's bingo activity is not unrelated business income because it qualifies for the bingo games exception.

Example: Sycamore church also sells scratch-off tickets during its Friday bingo nights in Busy City. Players *buy individual "$100 Bingo" scratch-off tickets in the hope that each one is a winner. Most tickets are losers. Selling scratch-off tickets is legal in Busy City, but only for nonprofit organizations and the state government. Income from the sale of the scratch-off tickets does not qualify for the bingo games exception, since the scratch-off game does not meet the legal definition of bingo. It does not matter that the game is labeled "$100 Bingo." The determination of whether the income is unrelated business income to the church would have to be made based on the regular definition of unrelated business income and other possible exceptions.*

Example: *Hemlock Church conducts bingo games each Friday night in Conservative City, in which people buy bingo cards and try to be the first contestant to fill a row of spaces on the cards when numbers are called. The winner of each game wins a prize that is distributed at the event. Bingo is <u>not</u> legal in Conservative City, but local officials do not enforce the law. Income from the bingo activity does not qualify for the bingo games exception, since the bingo activity is not legal in Conservative City. It does not matter that the law is not enforced. The determination of whether the income is unrelated business income to the church would have to be made based on the regular definition of unrelated business income and other possible exceptions.*

3
Debt-Financed Income

The federal tax laws and regulations related to debt-financed income are quite technical and complex. A church that believes it may have debt-financed income or that wants to proactively prevent or minimize it should consult knowledgeable tax counsel as early in the process as possible. In many cases, good planning may reduce or eliminate a significant tax liability that could otherwise occur.

As stated in Chapter 2, investment income such as interest, dividends, rents, royalties, and capital gains are ordinarily excluded from unrelated business income. The ordinary exclusion does not apply, however, if such income is generated from "debt-financed property."

Debt-financed property

According to federal regulations, debt-financed property is property held to produce income (including a gain on sale) for which there is "acquisition indebtedness" at any time during the tax year or during the twelve-month period prior to the date the property is sold.

Acquisition indebtedness

Acquisition indebtedness is debt incurred:

- When acquiring or improving the property;

- Before acquiring or improving the property if the debt would not have been incurred were it not for the acquisition or improvement; or

- After acquiring or improving the property if:

    ◊ The debt would not have been incurred were it not for the acquisition or improvement; and

    ◊ Incurring the debt was reasonably foreseeable when the property was acquired or improved.

In other words, acquisition indebtedness is debt that is incurred because the church acquired or improved certain property, regardless of whether the debt was incurred before or at the time the church acquired or improved the property. Debt incurred _after_ the acquisition or improvement of certain property could also be acquisition indebtedness if it is incurred because of the acquisition or improvement _and_ it was "reasonably foreseeable" that the church would incur the debt when the property was acquired or improved.

Collateralization is not relevant

In determining whether debt is acquisition indebtedness,

it does not matter whether it is collateralized by the property in question. The relevant question is why the debt was incurred – not what serves as collateral for it.

> *Example:* A church has a campus in Town A and owns 20 acres of vacant land in neighboring Town B. The church has no outstanding debt. The church borrows $1 million to buy a new parcel of property near its campus in Town A. In doing so, the church uses the 20 acres it owns in Town B as collateral for the new loan. The new property it acquires in Town A is not mortgaged and does not serve as collateral for the new loan. The new loan represents acquisition indebtedness with respect to the newly acquired parcel, even though the newly acquired parcel is not collateral for the loan, because the debt was incurred to acquire the new parcel. The debt is <u>not</u> acquisition indebtedness with respect to the 20 acres in Town B, even though that 20-acre property is collateral for the loan, because the debt was incurred to acquire the new parcel, not the 20-acre parcel the church already owned.

Special rules for identification and tracing of indebtedness

Complex issues may arise in determining whether indebtedness was incurred in connection with the acquisition and improvement of property when debt is refinanced, consolidated with other debt, or when a borrower engages in other similar actions. Federal tax law contains rules governing the manner in which the identity of debt related to a specific property is tracked, or traced, when such transactions occur. The tracing rules and process are extremely complex and should definitely be addressed by knowledgeable tax counsel.

> **Example:** *First Church buys its first property in Year 1 for $1 million and incurs debt of $800,000 in doing so. In Year 2, First Church acquires a second parcel of land for $500,000. At the time First Church acquires the second parcel, the debt related to the first parcel has been paid down to $700,000. First Church obtains a new loan in the amount of $1.1 million to pay off the original loan and provide financing for the new property. $400,000 of the new loan (the additional principal borrowed) represents acquisition indebtedness with respect to the second parcel and $700,000 of it relates to the first property acquired. Subsequent principal payments on the combined note must be allocated between the two properties in conformity with federal tax rules for purposes of determining remaining acquisition indebtedness.*

Special exception for educational institutions

A special exception (effectively, an exemption) to the ordinary rules for acquisition indebtedness exists in the law for organizations that are specifically classified by the Internal Revenue Service as educational institutions and for certain organizations related to such educational institutions. An organization classified by the IRS as an educational institution should have an IRS determination letter indicating that the organization is described in Section 170(b)(1)(A)(ii) of the Internal Revenue Code. This exception would not apply to a church, but it might apply to an entity that is affiliated with a church, such as a school, if that entity is classified by the IRS as an educational institution. The special exception for educational institutions involves several technical criteria which must be met and which should be evaluated by tax counsel.

Exception for property used for exempt purposes

Property used by a church exclusively for exempt purposes is not debt-financed property, regardless of the existence of acquisition indebtedness. Additionally, if "substantially all" (85 percent or more) of the use of the property is substantially related to the church's exempt purposes, the property is excluded from debt-financed property. The measurement of exempt use and total use may be made by time, space, or a combination of the two. If a church uses property with acquisition indebtedness less than 85 percent for exempt purposes, the portion of the property used for exempt purposes is <u>not</u> debt-financed property and the remainder is, unless another exception in the law applies.

> *Example:* Second Church owns a building that it acquired with debt financing. The building has 10,000 square feet of space. The church uses all of the space for church activities except a 1,000 square foot space that it rents to a local restaurant. The building is not debt-financed property because the church uses 90 percent of the building for exempt purposes.

> *Example:* Second Church owns a building that it acquired with debt financing. The building has 10,000 square feet of space. The church uses all of the space for church activities except a 3,000 square foot space that it rents to a local restaurant. 7,000 square feet, or 70 percent of the building, is <u>not</u> debt-financed property. The 3,000 feet (30 percent) of the building rented to the restaurant is debt-financed property, and the rental income received is debt-financed income unless another exception in the law applies.

Sale of debt-financed property not used for exempt purposes

A church can incur a significant tax liability if it sells debt-financed property that is not used for exempt purposes and generates a gain from the sale. This is an often-overlooked area of the law.

> **Example:** *Oak Church buys a vacant parcel of land for $1 million in Year 1, incurring debt in the amount of $800,000 in so doing with the intent of using the property for exempt purposes at some time in the future. The church never uses the property for exempt purposes. In Year 10, Oak Church sells the property for $10 million at a time when the remaining acquisition indebtedness is $500,000. Oak Church will incur a substantial tax liability related to its $9 million gain.*

Exception for property used in certain activities

Debt-financed property does not include property that is used to conduct any of the following activities for which the income is exempt from unrelated business income (See Chapter 2 for descriptions of these activities):

- A trade or business in which substantially all of the work is performed by persons who are not compensated for their work (the "volunteer exception");

- A trade or business conducted primarily for the convenience of the charity's members, students, officers, or employees (the "convenience of members exception"); or

- A trade or business that consists of selling merchandise, substantially all of which was received by the charity as gifts or contributions (the "donated goods exception").

The neighborhood land rule exception

If a church acquires property with debt financing and intends to use the land for exempt purposes within 15 years of the acquisition date, the property will not be considered debt-financed property. This special rule applies only if the plan to use the property for exempt purposes requires demolition of any buildings or structures on the property. A church relying on the neighborhood land rule to exclude rental income from debt-financed income may not abandon its plan to convert the land to exempt use. In the event the church does abandon its plan, the neighborhood land rule exception fails to apply from that point forward.

Additionally, if the church has not converted the land to exempt use within five years of the acquisition date, the church must notify the IRS that it is relying on the neighborhood land rule at the end of the fifth year and provide to the IRS information and documents supporting its claimed intent. The IRS will rule as to whether the church may continue to rely on the neighborhood land rule for the remainder of the allowable period (up to a total of 15 years). Even if the IRS does not rule favorably on the request, if the church ultimately does convert the land to exempt use within the allowable period in conformity with the neighborhood land rule, the rule will apply retroactively as if the IRS issued a favorable ruling at the end of the fifth year.

Special note regarding unique treatment for churches

The neighborhood land rule is so-named because in order for it to apply to exempt organizations other than churches, the property acquired must be in the "neighborhood" of the organization's existing exempt-use property. That rule does not apply to churches. Additionally, the maximum allowable period for which the neighborhood land rule can apply for non-church organizations is 10 years, instead of the 15-year period that applies to churches.

As is the case with other aspects of the debt-financed income rules, the neighborhood land rule involves a number of technical requirements and conditions that should be assessed by knowledgeable tax counsel.

> **Example:** *Pine Church acquires an office building with debt financing at the beginning of Year 1 and rents the office space to commercial tenants. Pine Church intends to demolish the office building before the end of Year 15 and construct a new education building on the property to be used exclusively for exempt purposes. At the end of Year 5, Pine Church notifies the IRS of its intent and provides the IRS with plans and drawings showing its progress toward using the property for exempt purposes within the allowable 15-year period. The IRS issues a ruling stating that Pine Church may continue to rely on the neighborhood land rule through Year 15. At the beginning of Year 12, the office building is demolished and Pine Church builds an education building on the property which is used exclusively for exempt purposes. The rental income received by Pine Church for the entire 11-year*

period prior to demolition is not debt-financed income because of the neighborhood land rule.

Example: *Pine Church acquires an office building with debt financing at the beginning of Year 1 and rents the office space to commercial tenants. Pine Church intends to demolish the office building before the end of Year 15 and construct a new education building on the property to be used exclusively for exempt purposes. At the end of Year 5, Pine Church notifies the IRS of its intent and provides the IRS with plans and drawings showing its progress toward using the property for exempt purposes within the allowable 15-year period. The IRS does not issue a favorable ruling stating that Pine Church may continue to rely on the neighborhood land rule through Year 15. Pine Church begins to treat its rental income from the property as debt-financed income starting in Year 6. At the beginning of Year 12, the office building is demolished and Pine Church builds an education building on the property which is used exclusively for exempt purposes. The rental income received by Pine Church for the entire 11-year period prior to demolition is not debt-financed income because of the neighborhood land rule. Since the church treated the income as debt-financed income for Years 6 through 11, the church may file amended returns and obtain a refund of all taxes paid on the income during that period.*

Calculation of debt-financed income subject to tax

In most cases, not all of the net income generated from debt-financed property is actually taxable. The amount that is taxable is based on the amount of applicable debt and the church's basis in the property.

Calculation of unrelated debt-financed income from regular activity (such as rental income)

In determining how much income (such as rental income) is actually unrelated debt-financed income with respect to a specific property, the church needs to know the <u>average</u> amount of acquisition indebtedness that was outstanding during the applicable tax year and the <u>average</u> tax basis (as defined in the Regulations) of the property for the period during the tax year that it held the property. The amount of the rental income that is considered unrelated debt-financed income is determined by multiplying the rental income by the ratio of the average acquisition indebtedness to the average tax basis of the property.

> **Example:** *Hickory Church owns a building that is debt-financed and rents it to a commercial tenant for $100,000 per year. For the year XXX4, Hickory Church had average acquisition indebtedness related to the building of $600,000 and its average tax basis for the building was $1 million. The ratio of the average acquisition indebtedness to the average tax basis is 60 percent. Therefore, 60 percent of the rental income, or $60,000, is considered unrelated gross debt-financed income. The church would also apply the 60 percent ratio to allowable expenses associated with the building's rental activity to determine the expenses that are deductible against the gross revenue of $60,000 in arriving at net unrelated taxable income (or loss) from the activity.*

Calculation of unrelated debt-financed income from the sale of property

In determining how much gain from the sale of debt-financed property is actually unrelated debt-financed income with respect to the property, the church needs to know the <u>highest</u> amount of acquisition indebtedness that was outstanding during the twelve-month period preceding the date of the sale and the <u>average</u> tax basis (as defined in the Regulations) of the property for the period during the tax year that it held the property. The amount of gain that is considered unrelated debt-financed income is determined by multiplying the gain from the sale by the ratio of the highest acquisition indebtedness to the average tax basis of the property.

> **Example:** *Oak Church buys a vacant parcel of land for $1 million in Year 1, incurring debt in the amount of $800,000 in so doing with the intent of using the property for exempt purposes at some time in the future. The church never uses the property for exempt purposes. At the end of Year 10, Oak Church sells the property for $10 million. The church's acquisition indebtedness related to the property was $600,000 at the beginning of Year 10 and had been paid down to $500,000 by the end of Year 10 when the property was sold. The church's average tax basis for the property was its original purchase price of $1 million. The church has a gain on the sale of the property of $9 million (the difference between the sales price of $10 million and the church's basis for the property of $1 million). The highest acquisition indebtedness related to the property during Year 10 was $600,000. The ratio of the highest acquisition*

indebtedness to the average tax basis is 60 percent. Therefore, 60 percent of the gain (or $5.4 million) is taxable as unrelated debt-financed income. (At current regular federal corporate tax rates, the federal income tax on the gain would be approximately $1.8 million. It is likely that state corporate income tax would also apply.)

Planning pointer: *If Oak Church had paid off the acquisition debt 13 months before it closed on the sale of the property, none of the gain would have been taxable. This is an example where good tax planning could have resulted in very substantial tax savings!*

4

Is Unrelated Business Income Really Such a Bad Thing?

Many churches try to avoid unrelated business income like the plague! But is UBI really such a bad thing? One positive theory is that it is better to have additional income, even if you have to pay some tax on it, than not to have the income at all. While such reasoning is logical, there are several implications associated with generating unrelated business income that a church should carefully consider in deciding whether to do so.

Federal and state filing requirements and tax rates

When a church generates more than $1,000 of gross revenue from unrelated business activities, the church is required to file a federal income tax return (Form 990-T). Form 990-T is due by the 15th day of the 5th month after the church's year-end (May 15 for a church operating on the calendar year) and may be extended for up to six months.

On Form 990-T, the church reports the revenue from its unrelated business activities and the expenses related to generating the revenue are deducted. If the revenue exceeds the deductible expenses, the church has net income from its unrelated business activities, which is subject to federal tax. If the church is incorporated (that is, it is a corporation, as are most churches in the U.S.) the regular U.S. corporate income tax rates apply.

Most states require a church that files Form 990-T to file a state income tax return as well, and if the church generates net income as calculated under state law, the church will likely also owe state income taxes calculated at applicable state income tax rates.

Implications for state and local taxes other than income taxes

When a church engages in any trade or business activity, whether it generates unrelated business income or not, it should consider the possible tax implications in state and local jurisdictions. For example, selling goods or services may subject the church to state sales tax laws, requiring the church to collect and remit sales tax on transactions subject to the tax. Renting property to tenants may result in similar obligations.

Laws in some states that provide property tax exemptions for churches require that property be used exclusively for exempt purposes in order to qualify for exemption. Where that is the case, a church that engages in a trade or business activity or that rents out its property to others should determine whether the conduct of the activity could adversely affect its exemption. The definition of exempt use of property for property tax exemption purposes is state-specific and is often different from the definition of exempt-purpose activity under federal income tax law.

It is possible, therefore, that engaging in <u>any</u> trade or business, including an unrelated business activity, could adversely affect a church's exemptions under various state or local laws and ordinances.

Calculating and minimizing net unrelated business income

Once a church determines that it has more than $1,000 of gross revenue from one or more unrelated business activities, it must determine its net taxable unrelated business income (or loss). Many organizations that have significant revenue from unrelated business activities actually generate a net loss from the activities after taking into account deductible expenses.

Chapter 3 addresses the manner in which unrelated debt-financed income is calculated.

To calculate net unrelated business income from other activities, the starting point is gross unrelated business revenue. Allowable expenses attributable to the unrelated business activities are deducted from gross revenue. In addition to expenses incurred by the church, the law allows a standard deduction of up to $1,000 (but the standard deduction cannot create a net loss or make a net loss larger).

In order to be allowable as deductions, expenses must be "directly connected" with carrying on the church's unrelated business activities. Some expenses are attributable solely to an unrelated business activity, and the relationship is straightforward. A church may incur some expenses that are attributable partly to unrelated business activities and partly to exempt activities, in which case a reasonable allocation must be made, and only that portion of the expense attributable to the unrelated business activity is deductible.

A church that engages in unrelated business activities should carefully evaluate all of its expenses to identify every expense that may be properly and reasonably allocated to and deducted from the unrelated business revenue. When all such expenses are identified and deducted, including a reasonably allocable portion of administrative and overhead expenses, the result is often a net loss.

Net losses from unrelated business activities may be carried back or forward to offset net income in other years in the same manner that is allowed under federal tax law for taxable corporations.

Can a church have too much unrelated business activity?

A church may not devote a substantial amount of its time, resources, or activities to any non-exempt purposes. Accordingly, if a substantial portion of a church's activities are dedicated to the conduct of one or more unrelated business activities, the church can lose its federal tax-exempt status under Section 501(c)(3) of the Internal Revenue Code. Unfortunately, the law is not clear with respect to measuring or determining the limits of unrelated business activity. The conclusions reached in various cases and rulings over the years vary dramatically due to the unique facts and circumstances in each of them. Many tax practitioners suggest that when a tax-exempt organization generates more than about 15 percent of its revenue from unrelated business activities, it should carefully consider (together with knowledgeable tax counsel) whether it may be exposed to risk of loss of exemption. An insubstantial amount of unrelated business activity is not a threat to a church's federal tax-exempt status.

5
Generating Income from Activities without Generating Unrelated Business Income

Churches may generate income from a variety of sources other than contributions without generating unrelated business income. Using the information described in the previous chapters regarding the definition of unrelated business income and the exceptions and exclusions that apply, a church can wisely plan its revenue-generating activities to avoid UBI treatment. Following are examples of income-generating activities in which a church may engage along with descriptions of how to avoid unrelated business income in conducting them.

Bookstores and gift shops

The volunteer exception

Income from a church bookstore or gift shop may be excluded entirely from unrelated business income if the activity is conducted substantially entirely (more than 85 percent) by volunteers (uncompensated workers). If the activity qualifies for the volunteer exception, it doesn't matter whether the items sold in the store or shop are substantially related to the church's exempt purposes or not; nor does it matter whether the store or shop is located on the church's property. When the volunteer exception applies, the activity may be conducted in a regular commercial location without affecting the exemption from unrelated business income.

Selling substantially related items

If all the items sold in the store or shop are of a nature that selling them contributes importantly to one or more of the church's exempt purposes, the activity will not generate unrelated business income. In some cases, the relationship between an item being sold and the church's exempt purposes may be obvious (e.g., Bibles, prayer books, worship music, etc.). As described in Chapter 1, in cases where the relationship is not obvious, the church should maintain adequate documentation to support the relationship between each item or category of similar items sold and the specific exempt purposes of the church.

Selling at off-site locations, through catalogues, and so on

Despite popular perception, a church bookstore does not have to be located on the church's property, operated with limited hours, or concealed from the public in order to have its activities qualify for exemption. In fact, a church selling items that are substantially related to its exempt purposes may operate its store or shop in a commercial location, be open during regular commercial hours, promote itself to the public, sell its items in mail-order catalogues or over the Internet, and use other similar methods of promotion without generating unrelated business income. In an authoritative ruling issued in the context of a museum selling substantially related greeting cards, the IRS clearly addressed the issue:

The organization sells the cards in the shop it operates in the museum. It also publishes a catalogue in which it solicits mail orders for the greeting cards. The catalogue is available at a small charge and is advertised in magazines and other publications throughout the year. In addition, the shop sells the cards at quantity discounts to retail stores. As a result, a large volume of cards are sold at a significant profit.

The museum is exempt as an educational organization on the basis of its ownership, maintenance, and exhibition for public viewing of works of art. The sale of greeting cards displaying printed reproductions of art works contributes importantly to the achievement of the museum's exempt educational purposes by stimulating and enhancing public awareness, interest, and appreciation of art. Moreover, a broader segment of the public may be encouraged to visit the museum itself to share in its educational functions and programs as a result of seeing the cards. The fact that the cards are promoted and sold in a clearly commercial manner at a profit and in competition with commercial greeting card publishers does not alter the fact of the activity's relatedness to the museum's exempt purpose. *(Revenue Ruling 73-104 – Emphasis added.)*

The IRS subsequently reaffirmed the conclusion it reached in the Revenue Ruling cited above when it issued a Technical Advice Memorandum (TAM) in a museum context. The question at hand was whether off-site sales by the museum of substantially related items constituted unrelated business activity. In the TAM, in which the museum is referred to as "M," the IRS stated:

> M carries on extensive off-site sales activities. It uses several vehicles to accomplish these sales: retail stores, gift shops, an outlet located in another city, mail-order catalogues, advertisements in various other publications, corporate/conference program, etc. Clearly, M has developed an off-site outlet network and receives significant revenue from such sales.

> It is, therefore, not unreasonable to infer from this that the purpose behind the off-site sales activities is a commercial one. Were this not an exempt organization, such logic would be persuasive. <u>However, regarding the sale of related items by an exempt organization, Rev. Rul. 73-104 holds that neither the proximity of the sale to the museum's location nor the fact that the individual purchaser never sets foot on the property matters.</u>

> In Rev. Rul. 73-104, the organization sold large volumes of cards at quantity discounts to retail stores and through its mail order catalogues. The revenue ruling states the following: "The fact that the greeting cards are promoted and sold in a clearly commercial manner at a profit and in competition with commercial greeting card publishers does not alter the fact of the activity's relatedness to the museum's exempt purpose." <u>Thus, once it is determined</u>

that a line of merchandise is related to the purposes of a museum, the broader the market the museum is able to reach, the more it can fulfill its exempt function. ... Therefore, exempt product sales occurring outside the Museum Site do not (for that reason alone) constitute unrelated trade or business under section 513 of the Code. *(TAM 9550003 – Emphasis added. While a TAM is not authoritative, it is helpful in understanding the IRS's position on a particular issue.)*

A church that wishes to engage in aggressive, commercial-type sales of items that it believes are substantially related to its exempt purposes should obtain advice from tax counsel to ensure that it is in compliance with the law. Depending on the volume and scope of the activity, it may be wise to obtain a private ruling from the IRS.

Parking lots

The IRS has consistently held that the operation of a revenue-producing parking lot by an exempt organization is not a rental of real estate, but rather is a trade or business activity. As is the case with other trade or business activities, a church may operate a parking lot in a manner where substantially all (more than 85 percent) of the work is performed by volunteers and the operation will be exempt from the tax on unrelated business income.

As an alternative, the church could rent the property on which the parking lot sits to an unrelated parking company and the parking company could operate the parking lot. In that scenario, the revenue to the church is real estate rental income, which is not unrelated business income (unless the property is debt-financed). Even if the property is debt-financed, the church should consider whether it may qualify for:

- The substantially exempt use exception, or

- The neighborhood land rule exclusion, if the church plans to convert the property to exempt use within 15 years of the date it was acquired.

(See Chapter 3 for a description of these exceptions.)

Concerts or other special events

The conduct of revenue-generating concerts or other events by a church will not generate unrelated business income if the event itself contributes importantly to one or more of the church's exempt purposes. The relationship between the event and the church's exempt purposes (e.g., worship, evangelism, etc.) should be well-documented to support the church's position. Again, as with other trade or business activities, conducting substantially all of the activity by volunteers will also result in the income being exempt from the tax on unrelated business income.

Thrift shops or other sales of donated merchandise

As described in Chapter 2, a trade or business of selling merchandise is not an unrelated business activity if "substantially all" of the merchandise sold is donated to the church. Court cases and rulings indicate that "substantially all" for this purpose means 85 percent or more of the merchandise sold. Therefore, the operation of a thrift shop selling donated goods is not an unrelated business activity.

Similarly, the sale of donated merchandise using other methods (such as online auctions, including eBay) is not an unrelated business activity. (Note: A portion of eBay's website is dedicated specifically to online sales by nonprofit organizations.)

Corporate sponsorship of events

Also as described extensively in Chapter 2, revenue received by a church as payment for a qualified sponsorship activity is not unrelated business income. A qualified sponsorship activity is an activity in which an outside party (typically a business) pays a church to sponsor an event or activity conducted by the church and receives in exchange certain limited types of recognition or acknowledgment. As long as the acknowledgment or recognition made by the church of the sponsor meets certain criteria, and the church does not provide the sponsor with a "substantial return benefit," the transaction constitutes a qualified sponsorship activity. (See the detailed description and examples of qualified sponsorship arrangements in Chapter 2.)

Scrip programs

Scrip programs are activities in which an organization purchases gift cards (or their equivalent) at a discount and then sells them to supporters, often for face value. For example, a church might purchase $100 gift cards from a grocery chain at a price of $90 each and sell them to church members for $100 each. Since the members are able to use the cards to buy $100 of groceries, the scrip program is an appealing way to raise money. Ordinarily, the regular operation of a scrip program by a church would constitute an unrelated business activity. The IRS has ruled, however, that when the volunteer exception applies (i.e., when substantially all of the activity is conducted by volunteers) the activity is not an unrelated business activity.

Coffee shops and cafés

The best way for a church to avoid having a coffee shop or café treated as an unrelated business activity is to limit its activity to providing service in connection with events on the church's property. Doing so will help the church take advantage of the "convenience of members" exemption described in Chapter 2. If the church wants to have a full-service coffee shop or café open to the public for regular business hours, it should consider having the activity conducted substantially entirely by volunteers to avoid unrelated business income.

Alternatively, the church could rent a portion of its real property to an unrelated company to operate the coffee shop or café on the site. If the property is not debt-financed, real estate rental income is not unrelated business income. If the church's real property is debt-financed, the church should determine whether an exception may apply to the debt-financed income rules, such as the rule described in Chapter 3 that exempts debt-financed income if substantially all (85 percent or more) of the property is used for exempt purposes.

About the Author

Michael E. (Mike) Batts has served on, chaired, and consulted with nonprofit boards for more than 25 years. His board service has included serving as the board chairman for ECFA, a national nonprofit accrediting organization for religious nonprofit organizations in the areas of board governance and financial integrity. Mike was recently appointed chairman of the Commission on Accountability and Policy for Religious Organizations, a national commission convened upon the request of U.S. Senator Charles Grassley to address accountability and policy issues for U.S. religious organizations. Mike previously served on the Legal Framework Workgroup of the Panel on the Nonprofit Sector, an advisory panel to the U.S. Senate Finance Committee convened at the request of Senator Charles Grassley. He was first drawn to serving nonprofit organizations in response to his Christian faith and the need he saw among nonprofit organizations for guidance in the area of board governance and compliance.

Mike is also a CPA and the managing shareholder of Batts Morrison Wales & Lee, P.A., an Orlando-based CPA firm dedicated exclusively to serving nonprofit organizations and their affiliates throughout the United States.

Mike speaks throughout the country and writes frequently on topics related to the nonprofit sector. He is also active legislatively, having drafted and lobbied successfully for a number of changes to laws affecting nonprofit organizations.